SANDRA BULLOCK

A Real-Life Reader Biography

Susan Zannos

Mitchell Lane Publishers, Inc.
P.O. Box 619 • Bear, Delaware 19701

First Printing

Real-Life Reader Biographies

Selena	Robert Rodriguez	Mariah Carey	Rafael Palmeiro
Tommy Nuñez	Trent Dimas	Cristina Saralegui	Andres Galarraga
Oscar De La Hoya	Gloria Estefan	Jimmy Smits	Mary Joe Fernandez
Cesar Chavez	Chuck Norris	Sinbad	Paula Abdul
Vanessa Williams	Celine Dion	Mia Hamm	Sammy Sosa
Brandy	Michelle Kwan	Rosie O'Donnell	Shania Twain
Garth Brooks	Jeff Gordon	Mark McGwire	Salma Hayek
Sheila E.	Hollywood Hogan	Ricky Martin	Britney Spears
Arnold Schwarzenegger	Jennifer Lopez	Kobe Bryant	Derek Jeter
Steve Jobs	**Sandra Bullock**	Julia Roberts	Robin Williams
Jennifer Love Hewitt	Keri Russell	Sarah Michelle Gellar	Liv Tyler
Melissa Joan Hart	Drew Barrymore	Alicia Silverstone	Katie Holmes
Winona Ryder	Alyssa Milano		

Library of Congress Cataloging-in-Publication Data
Zannos, Susan.
    Sandra Bullock / Susan Zannos.
        p. cm. — (A real-life reader biography)
    Includes Index.
    Filmography:
    ISBN 1-58415-027-0
    1. Bullock, Sandra—Juvenile Literature. 2. Motion picture actors and actresses—United States—Biography—Juvenile literature. [1. Bullock, Sandra. 2. Actors and actresses. 3. Women—Biography.] I. Title. II. Series.
    PN2287.B737 Z36 2000
    791.43′028′092—dc21

                                                                                    00-036531

ABOUT THE AUTHOR: Susan Zannos has taught at all levels, from preschool to college, in Mexico, Greece, Italy, Russia, and Lithuania, as well as in the United States. She has published a mystery *Trust the Liar* (Walker and Co.) and *Human Types: Essence and the Enneagram* was published by Samuel Weiser in 1997. She has written several books for children, including *Paula Abdul* and *Cesar Chavez* (Mitchell Lane).
PHOTO CREDITS: Cover: Kobal Collection; p. 4 Kobal Collection; p. 6 Globe Photos; p. 8 Kobal Collection; p. 12 Archive Photos; p. 18, 22 Kobal Collection; p. 24 Joyce Rudolph/Fotos International/Archive Photos; p. 28 Reuters/Handout/Archive Photos; p. 29 Globe Photos
ACKNOWLEDGMENTS: The following story has been thoroughly researched, and to the best of our knowledge, represents a true story. While every possible effort has been made to ensure accuracy, the publisher will not assume liability for damages caused by inaccuracies in the data, and makes no warranty on the accuracy of the information contained herein.

Table of Contents

Chapter 1   Gypsy Child 5

Chapter 2   Bartender 10

Chapter 3   Starlet 15

Chapter 4   Star 20

Chapter 5   Businesswoman............................. 25

Filmography 31

Chronology 32

Index 32

4

Chapter 1
Gypsy Child

Sandra Bullock got an early start in her acting career. Her parents were both opera singers. Sandra's father, who came from Alabama, was the youngest of eight children. He worked as a blacksmith to earn money to attend the famous Juilliard School in New York City. He wanted to become an opera singer. John Bullock was working in Germany when he met Helga, a German opera singer.

Sandra was born to John and Helga Bullock in Washington, D.C., on July 26, 1964. When Sandra was little, her father

Sandra's parents were both opera singers.

Sandra with her parents.

worked as a voice coach. Helga's singing career in Austria and Germany was doing well, so Sandra traveled with her mother to Germany for the opera seasons. Sandra says, "The opera is a great baby-sitting service. In just about any opera, there's a dirty gypsy child in the background. That was my part. My mother would shove me upstage and say, 'Stay there.'" It was Sandra's first taste of acting, and she liked it. She also spent a lot of time in the costume department with the wardrobe woman.

While they were in Germany, Sandra and her mother lived with her aunt and grandmother in Nuremberg, where Sandra went to the local schools. She had a tutor in English in the afternoons so that she wouldn't fall behind in her American schoolwork. Sandra still speaks German fluently.

Sandra took ballet and piano lessons, but she was also a tomboy. Her younger sister, Gesine, was born when Sandra was five years old. While her mother was busy with the baby, Sandra spent a lot of time puttering around with her dad, helping him fix things. She still has a scar from slipping on rocks and falling into a creek while she and her father were hiking together when she was 11 years old.

When she was in elementary school, Sandra liked the gypsy life of traveling back and forth to Germany and performing. By the time she was in sixth grade, she knew she wanted to be an actor. Later, coming back from Europe when she was in junior high, it was hard for her to fit in with the other kids at school. "Being thirteen is hard anyway," Sandra says, "and here I was, not being the same as everybody else."

Although her mother kept telling her that she didn't need to be like

By the time she was in sixth grade, Sandra knew she wanted to be an actor.

7

When Sandra was young, she wanted to be like the other kids her age.

everyone else, for Sandra it was important to be accepted by other kids her age. She didn't want to travel anymore. She didn't want her parents to be opera singers. That was too unusual. Sandra said later, "When other kids would hear the lessons going on in the house, it was so embarrassing. My sister and I would think, *Please, can you tone it down a little?* We wanted them banned to the closet."

The Bullock family settled in Arlington, Virginia, where Sandra went to Washington-Lee High School. She was popular there. She was a cheerleader, and her 1982 senior yearbook named her class clown. The senior class voted her Most Likely to Brighten Your Day. Sandra's classmates remember her as being able to make anyone laugh. One friend from high school remembers, "She wasn't smoking or wearing ripped clothes. She didn't do drugs. She was an above-average student, but no brainiac."

In spite of Sandra's cheerful disposition and clowning around, she was still serious about becoming an actor. When she graduated from high school, she decided to go to East Carolina University in North Carolina to study drama. Her acting teacher remembers the intensity with which she performed. He says, "I remember thinking, 'She is fearless.'"

Sandra left college before she completed her degree. She had only a few more classes to take before graduating, but she decided to head for New York. She explains, "There's so much fear of failure in me that if I think too much about something, I won't do it, so I sort of do things blindly. I packed up my little Honda Accord and my little dog and put all my junk in the hatchback, and I went."

Sandra decided to go to East Carolina University to study drama.

Sandra was a hopeful young actor when she arrived in New York in 1985.

Every year, hundreds of hopeful young actors from all over the United States head for New York City. Maybe they had been in their senior-class play in high school. Maybe they had studied in the drama departments of small colleges or large universities. They think they're ready for the big time. They're ready to become stars. They're ready to see their names up in lights on Broadway theaters.

Sandra Bullock was one of these hopeful young actors when she arrived in New York in 1985. She was 21 years old. She had a place to live because her father kept an apartment where he would sometimes give music lessons. "It wasn't plush," Sandra says, "but I don't need a lot of things."

She had the support of her parents. They knew from their own experience how hard it is to have a career in the arts. They had struggled to succeed and they expected their daughter would do the same. They said, "Whatever you do, do it a hundred percent."

Sandra got a job as a bartender. Although she didn't have any experience, she said she did. "I didn't know how to mix any fancy drinks," she admitted. "The customers helped me." With this job she was able to support herself so that she could study Method acting with a good drama teacher, Sanford Meisner. She also watched the ads in *Backstage* magazine to find out about open auditions.

At this point Sandra was no different from all the others. They all had to take night jobs as waiters or

Sandra's parents knew from their own experience how hard it is to have a career in the arts.

Sandra would go to many open auditions to try out for small parts.

waitresses, security guards, or janitors so that they could study and go to casting calls and open auditions during the day. When open auditions were held, anyone could try out for the part. There would be dozens of unknown actors competing for each small role in a play.

Sandra had spent her time in college studying different styles and methods of acting. In New York she decided, "I'm going to just barge in and audition." She admitted later, "I made a lot of mistakes. I didn't know what I was doing, but I had to learn somehow. There's so much rejection. If you take it to heart, you're lost."

It was very hard to keep trying. It was hard to work long hours at a demanding job at night and then get up early to study and go to auditions. It was also hard to face rejections week after week. Most of the young people who go to New York dreaming of acting careers give up after a while. They settle for other jobs or they go back to their hometowns. Sandra didn't give up.

One of Sandra's close friends, who is also an actor, said, "The thing that set her apart from all the other pretty, talented girls was that she worked hard. . . . Whether it was a side job to make extra money or preparing for an audition, she always went the extra mile. She had that German work ethic, and it's paid off."

Sandra admits that she almost gave up. Almost, but not quite. "There was only one time when I said I was going to quit this business, in my early twenties," she says. "I said I would give it one more year, but I didn't think I'd make it work. [My career] was out of my control, and I'm a control freak."

She finally got the break she needed in 1988 when she landed the part of a Southern belle in an off-

It was hard for Sandra to face rejections week after week.

Broadway play called *No Time Flat*. The play received bad reviews and soon closed, but well-known theater critic John Simon praised Sandra's performance. Taking the review with her, Sandra managed to get an agent.

Getting an agent is a very important step in beginning an acting career. All hopeful young actors try hard to get an agent. Having an agent means that an actor no longer has to spend long hours at open auditions. The agent knows what parts are available and will arrange audition appointments. The agent knows the directors and producers and will try to interest them in the actor.

Sandra's agent was able to help her get small parts in two 1989 made-for-TV movies.

Sandra's agent was able to help her get small parts in two 1989 made-for-TV movies, *Bionic Showdown* and *The Preppie Murder*. With these two acting credits in films, Sandra decided it was time to move to California.

Chapter 3
Starlet

Some hopeful young actors move to New York and others move to Los Angeles. Usually, like Sandra Bullock, they wait until they have at least one or two film credits and an agent before trying their luck in Hollywood.

Sandra had a friend to stay with in the Valley, the northeastern part of L.A. She says, "I had a rent-a-wreck, and I'd drive over the canyons every day to audition, and the car wouldn't go more than twenty miles an hour. So I'm sputtering up Bel Air Canyon, putt putt putt, and all these Jaguars are blowing

Sandra had a friend to stay with in the Valley, the north-eastern part of L.A.

their horns, and I'm like, 'Hey, I'm sorry, I'm just trying to make an honest living here.'"

Sandra did get some work. Like many other beginning actors, she got some television work and some roles in movies made for the video market. She was a starlet, a baby star—but she wasn't known by audiences and wasn't in demand by directors and producers. In 1990 she got the lead part in a TV series based on the movie *Working Girl.* She played the part of an ambitious secretary. The series didn't do well with reviewers or in the ratings; it lasted only six weeks. Sandra also made a movie called *Fire on the Amazon.* When she found out the script required her to do a nude scene, she was so upset she threw up when the scene was over. She called that period "my season in hell."

Then, in 1991, she was cast as the female lead in a movie called *Love Potion No. 9.* The male lead was Tate Donovan, another young actor trying his luck in Los Angeles. Tate's background was

In 1991, Sandra was cast as the female lead in a movie called *Love Potion No. 9.*

similar to Sandra's. He'd been born on the East Coast, studied acting at the University of Southern California, and appeared in a few movies that no one ever saw.

Love Potion No. 9 was a romantic comedy about two nerdy and lonely scientists. A gypsy fortune-teller gives them a love potion, love potion no. 8. The scientists decide to test it as an experiment. It works! They go from being homely and awkward, to both becoming attractive and self-confident, gaining crowds of admirers. Of course they realize that they are really in love with each other, thanks to a more powerful love potion, love potion no. 9.

The plot is both silly and predictable. The critics didn't like the movie at all, even though Sandra Bullock did a great job of changing from a really ugly and insecure drudge to an elegant and beautiful young lady. The movie wasn't a success, but the love potion was. Sandra Bullock and Tate Donovan fell in love.

The movie wasn't a success, but the love potion was.

Sandra's first big break was when she was hired for a role in Demolition Man.

Sandra's career started picking up in 1992. She got a series of good supporting roles. She played a kidnapping victim in a thriller *The Vanishing* with Jeff Bridges and Kiefer Sutherland. She played a lonely waitress in *Wrestling Ernest Hemingway*, a movie that critics liked, but that didn't do well at the box office. Sandra said about this film, "I love small, noncommercial films. . . . Richard Harris and Robert Duvall played these two old guys at the end of their lives. They're on the loneliness road, and I played a waitress who was lonely too, trying to find her way. . . . I hope people rent it."

In 1993 Sandra acted in two movies, *When the Party's Over* and *The Thing Called Love.*

Meanwhile, Sandra and Tate Donovan continued dating, and she was very much in love with him. She said at the time, "It's like they say, there's one person in your life, and Tate and I are closer than any two people I've ever experienced in my life. There's nobody that means more to me, and I know for a fact that I mean the most to him, in that certain way."

Tate Donovan's career wasn't doing well, but Sandra's was. Her first big break came when the actress playing in Sylvester Stallone's film *Demolition Man* was fired a few days after they started shooting. The producer heard about Sandra and was impressed by her audition tape. After a brief meeting, he hired her. Even though *Demolition Man* didn't do well immediately (it later did very well on video), it established Sandra Bullock as an actress with diverse abilities.

The producer of *Demolition Man* heard about Sandra and was impressed by her audition tape.

Chapter 4
Star

Friends advised Sandra not to try out for *Speed,* telling her she'd just be "the girl."

After playing the part of the eager young policewoman who helps Sylvester Stallone defeat Wesley Snipes in *Demolition Man,* Sandra Bullock was not interested in doing another action movie. But when she read the script for *Speed,* she changed her mind. She knew she wanted to play the part of the girl who drives the bus. Friends advised her not to try out for the part, telling her that she'd just be "the girl." But Sandra says, "I've learned to do things by instinct."

Her instinct told her the part was right for her. She knew that her chance of getting it depended on the way she got along with Keanu Reeves, who had already been signed for the male lead. When she went to audition, there were more than a dozen other actresses trying out for the part. When she saw Reeves, she says, "I thought he'd be this long-haired wild child, but I got in there and he was completely transformed. . . . This was not the person I'd thought he was."

When Sandra and Keanu read together, there was a good feeling between them.

The director wanted Sandra for the part. The studio executives did not. They wanted someone more glamorous, a blonde with a great figure and long legs. The director fought to have Sandra play the part. He finally won.

The girl on the bus, who is on her way to work, takes over for the bus driver when he is accidently shot by a frightened kid, who thinks the policeman, played by Keanu Reeves, has

There were more than a dozen other actresses trying out for the part.

Speed *was a hit at the box-office.*

boarded the bus to arrest him. The real reason the policeman is on the bus is that a madman has wired a bomb under it. The bomb will go off if the speed of the bus slows to less than 50 miles per hour. The character played by Sandra was taking the bus to work because her driver's license was revoked for too many speeding tickets. She doesn't mind driving fast, but that isn't easy on crowded Los Angeles freeways. While Sandra drives, Keanu Reeves attempts to disarm the bomb and out-think the madman.

When *Speed* opened at movie theaters in June 1994, it was a smash hit. It became a box-office blockbuster, taking in more than $300 million worldwide. It also made Sandra Bullock a star. The critics loved her. The audiences loved her. Sandra took a vacation. "I wanted to wait for a great project," she said. "That's difficult for an actor. . . . You think you'll never work again. But I'd worked nineteen months straight. I had nothing fresh to give another role, I was so burned out."

Sandra was burned out in her personal life, too. Her relationship with Tate Donovan ended. Her heart was broken and she needed time to grieve. After six months, however, Sandra moved on to her next hit, *While You Were Sleeping.* Playing the part of a lonely subway worker who saves the life of the man she has a crush on gave Sandra a chance to use her own loneliness in the role she was playing.

Her next movie was *The Net.* Sandra played the role of a computer expert who uncovers a computer crime. The hackers, people who figure out how to break into private computer programs, erase all evidence of her identity from the world's computers. Birth certificate, social security number,

Sandra had a chance to use her own loneliness in the role she was playing.

In The Net, *Sandra plays the part of a woman whose identity is erased by computer hackers.*

driver's record, passport—everything is gone. The hackers give her a new identity: one with a criminal record so that she'll be wanted by the police. Meanwhile, she is fighting for her life as the criminals try to kill her.

As her hit films kept bringing in big money at the box office, the amount she was paid for each movie got larger and larger. She had earned about $500,000 for *Speed*. Two years later, in 1996, she got $6 million for her supporting role as an eager young law student in *A Time to Kill*, and later that year $11 million for starring in *In Love and War*. Sandra Bullock had become one of the highest-paid women stars in Hollywood.

Chapter 5
Businesswoman

Being one of the biggest stars in Hollywood hasn't caused Sandra Bullock to fall for the glitz and glamour of the place. "I'm not what you call a hot tamale," she says. "There is something comfortable about me. I'm like a sleeper sofa. A good couch your grandmother has."

The image she projects in many of her roles is of confidence and competence. The policewoman in *Demolition Man*, the bus driver in *Speed*, the computer expert in *The Net*, and the law student in *A Time to Kill* are all able

> **The image Sandra projects in many of her roles is of confidence and competence.**

to take care of themselves and quite a bit else besides. These characters are more gutsy than glamorous, as practical as they are pretty.

The real Sandra Bullock is like that, too. Keeping her feet on the ground even though her career is rocketing into orbit is important to her. She renovated the older Spanish-style house she bought in a Los Angeles canyon, doing much of the work herself.

Renovating the house was therapy for her after her breakup with Tate Donovan. Her father flew out to Los Angeles to help. Sandra went to Mexico and bought hand-painted tiles, which she set in the kitchen floor herself while her father worked on the bathroom plumbing. Her sister, Gesine, who was then a law student, moved in with her and their three dogs.

On a movie set Sandra doesn't act the part of a big star. She not only gets her own coffee, but she brings coffee for the rest of the crew as well. For such glamorous Hollywood events as the

Renovating her house was therapy for Sandra.

premieres of her films, Sandra may show up with her parents, as she did for *While You Were Sleeping.* Her escort for the premiere of *The Net* was one of the technicians who had worked on the movie.

She wouldn't think her life was over if her acting career ended. She says, "I would redo houses, I would produce plays, I would do something. I'm like a shark. If I stop, I'll just die; if I keep moving, I'm okay." Her mother taught her to be practical and independent, saying, "You don't need a man to get you where you want to go. Make your own money, get your own career together, and then if you happen to meet a great guy, you'll meet him on a good level."

Sandra Bullock definitely has her career together. She decided in the mid-90's to be a good businesswoman. She said, "I don't want to be stupidly looking at a contract and saying, 'Okay, I'll sign it,' and later realizing I have nothing. So I've forced myself to be very

Sandra wouldn't think her life was over if her acting career ended.

The sequel to Speed *was a disappointment.*

smart business-wise." Sandra made some disap-pointing movies in 1996 and 1997. *Two If by Sea* and *In Love and War* did not do well at the box office, and the sequel to *Speed,* called *Speed 2: Cruise Control,* was a disaster. After that, Sandra took charge. She started her own production company, Fortis Films, with the help of her father and her sister, who was by then a lawyer.

Fortis Films' first production was *Hope Floats,* which many critics considered to be Sandra's best performance. She plays the part of a former cheerleader and prom queen who marries the high-school football hero and becomes a devoted wife and mother. She learns, on a television talk show, that her husband is in love with her best friend. She returns to her hometown and tries to put her life back together. *Hope Floats* made twice as much money as it cost to make, demonstrating that Sandra Bullock is indeed a very good businesswoman.

With the success of this film came more opportunities. In the same year, 1998, she starred as a witch in the big-budget film *Practical Magic,* with Nicole Kidman as her sister witch. Sandra also created the voice of Miriam for the animated feature *The Prince of Egypt.*

Hope Floats *was Fortis Films' first movie.*

In 1999 she costarred with Ben Affleck in the

successful romantic comedy *Forces of Nature.* Her production company, Fortis Films, released several films in 2000. In *Gun Shy* Sandra has the supporting role of a nurse who falls in love with a burned-out federal agent played by Liam Neeson. In *Miss Congeniality* she plays the role of an FBI agent who goes undercover at a beauty pagent.

Sandra's family and good friends know that she could be a gaffer, someone who builds the sets for movies, if she wanted to. She's already proven that she can be a movie producer. She wrote and performed her own country music for the movie *The Thing Called Love* and was the executive producer for the soundtrack of *Practical Magic.* She wrote and directed her own short film, *Making Sandwiches.* There really isn't much that Sandra Bullock can't do when it comes to making movies.

But her fans like to see her acting. Her lopsided smile and fresh-as-a-daisy good looks have captured everyone's heart.

Filmography

1987	*Hangmen*
1989	*Bionic Showdown: The Six-Million-Dollar Man and the Bionic Woman* (TV Movie)
	The Preppie Murder (TV Movie)
	Religion, Inc.
1990	*Who Shot Patakango?*
1991	*Fire on the Amazon*
1992	*Love Potion No. 9*
	Who Do I Gotta Kill?
1993	*The Vanishing*
	Wrestling Ernest Hemingway
	When the Party's Over
	The Thing Called Love
	Demolition Man
1994	*Speed*
1995	*While You Were Sleeping*
	The Net
1996	*Two If by Sea*
	A Time to Kill
	In Love and War
1997	*Speed 2: Cruise Control*
1998	*Welcome to Hollywood*
	Hope Floats
	Practical Magic
	The Prince of Egypt
	Making Sandwiches
1999	*Forces of Nature*
2000	*Gun Shy*
	Miss Congeniality
	Exactly 3:30
	28 Days

Chronology

- Born in Washington, D.C., on July 26, 1964
- Sister, Gesine, born in 1969
- Traveled between Virginia and Germany for the opera season in 1970-1977
- Graduated from Washington-Lee High School in Arlington, Virginia, 1982
- 1983, attended East Carolina University in Greenville, North Carolina
- 1985, moved to New York City and studied Method acting with Sanford Meisner
- Appeared in off-Broadway play *No Time Flat*; favorable review from critic John Simon in 1988
- In 1990, moved to Los Angeles; landed lead role in TV sitcom *Working Girl*
- Met actor Tate Donovan while costarring in *Love Potion No. 9 in 1991*
- Wrote and performed country music for *The Thing Called Love, 1993*
- 1994, became a star as bus-driving heroine of *Speed*; broke up with Tate Donovan
- 1995, bought and remodeled her own home in Los Angeles canyon area
- In 1996, became one of Hollywood's highest-paid women stars
- Formed her own production company, Fortis Films, in 1998
- 1999, nominated for People's Choice award as Favorite Motion Picture Actress

Index

Bullock, Gesine (sister) 7, 26
Bullock, Helga (mother) 5, 6, 7, 27
Bullock, John (father) 5, 7, 26
Bullock, Sandra
   agent 14
   auditions 12-13
   bartends 11
   birth of 5
   education of 6-9
   movies
      Bionic Showdown 14
      Demolition Man 19
      Fire on the Amazon 16

Hope Floats 28-29
Love Potion No. 9 16-17
Net, The 23-24
Practical Magic 29
Preppie Murder, The 14
Prince of Egypt, The 29
Speed 20-22
Vanishing, The 18
While You Were Sleeping 23
Wrestling Ernest Hemingway 18
Donovan, Tate 16-17, 19, 23
Fortis Films 28, 30
opera 5, 6